A–Z

OF

HALIFAX

PLACES - PEOPLE - HISTORY

Trish Colton

AMBERLEY

Acknowledgements

I would like to thank David Glover, Bryan Harkness, Tim Kirker, Bankfield Museum staff, John Hogg, Canon Hilary Barber, Chris Sutcliffe, Linda Pierson, Margaret Mattingley, Brian Drake, John Beazley, Diane Holloway and Bob Wood for their help in various ways.

First published 2020

Amberley Publishing
The Hill, Stroud, Gloucestershire, GL5 4EP
www.amberley-books.com

Copyright © Trish Colton, 2020

The right of Trish Colton to be identified as the Author of this work has been asserted in accordance with the Copyrights, Designs and Patents Act 1988.

ISBN 978 1 4456 7953 2 (print)
ISBN 978 1 4456 7954 9 (ebook)

British Library Cataloguing in Publication Data. A catalogue record for this book is available from the British Library.

Typesetting by Aura Technology and Software Services, India. Printed in Great Britain.

Contents

Introduction

There's an awful lot to write about where Halifax is concerned, from well-known landmarks such as our renovated Piece Hall and Anne Lister's Shibden Hall home, to the great mills that gave the town its early prosperity. Then there are the many famous personalities who come from Halifax: Anne Lister crops up again, so does Percy Shaw and his life-saving invention of cat's eyes, and a more modern inclusion could have been Ed Sheeran. Instead, I have tried to find subjects that are either less well known, or a different angle on a familiar topic. And still I found I had not got enough space for everything I should have liked to include. Even so, if you find yourself thinking 'I didn't know that', then I've achieved my main objective.

A

Antique Playing Card

When Robert Morden produced a set of playing cards in 1676, it is doubtful if he thought they would still be around 342 years later. In 2014 his set of playing cards was sold by Sotherby's for £15,000. The illustrations on the back of them were maps of different counties in England and Wales, including one of Yorkshire. Near the south-western edge of the map, is a dot with 'Halifax' beside it.

Sadly, not worth as much as Robert Morden's cards.

Antiquarian Society

In January 2018 a rare 'silver or silvered white metal' token was sold by the London auctioneers Spinks in their American showroom for three times its estimate. That coin once belonged to Samuel Henry Hamer, a Halifax numismatist described in the catalogue as 'a major collector of tokens at the turn of the 20th century'. Hamer also had a keen interest in local history.

Along with others who shared his interest in local history, he founded the Halifax Antiquarian Society in 1901. Its first president was John Lister MA of Shibden Hall, who encouraged the society's members to undertake enough research so that a comprehensive history of the town could be written. There had been two histories of Halifax published in the later eighteenth century, and another in 1836, but a new look at the town's history was obviously sorely needed.

Lister got his wish, but it took almost a century for it to make an appearance – and then the author was a Lancastrian! *Halifax* by Dr John A. Hargreaves is described as a 'full length history [which] explains the complex process by which 'a few straggling tenements built of wood, wattles and thatch … became the town we know today'.

Since 1901, local research has been undertaken by society members and others interested in the history of Calderdale, and the resulting articles are published annually by the society in their *Transactions of the Halifax Antiquarian Society*.

Antiquarian Society's logo.

B

Banks

Halifax was the birthplace of not one but two important banks that are still around today – both founded in the same decade. The first was Halifax Permanent Benefit Building and Investment Company, now known simply as the Halifax, founded in 1852. The other was Yorkshire Penny Bank, now called the Yorkshire Bank, founded in 1859.

The first person to be granted a mortgage by the Halifax was Esau Hanson, one of the bank's founders. He borrowed £121 (over £15,000 in today's money). The bank's former headquarters building on Trinity Road now stands on the land he borrowed that money for, so I imagine it is worth rather more than £15,000 in reality! At one

Worth much more now than when Esau Hanson bought the land.

point in its history, just before the First World War, its assets of £3 million meant it was the largest building society in the world.

After growing through various acquisitions and mergers, the Halifax was itself acquired by the Lloyds Banking Group in 2009, which then made Lloyds the largest retail bank in the UK.

Edward Akroyd was one of Halifax's wealthy industrial magnates who saw it as their philanthropic duty to help their workers and those less fortunate than themselves. As well as building houses for his factory workers to live in and several churches for the people of Halifax to worship in, he also provided a pension scheme for his employees.

To enable them to safely save small amounts of money as and when they could, rather than having to save larger amounts to invest, he founded a 'penny bank' in 1859 called the West Riding of Yorkshire Provident Society and Penny Savings Bank. Within two years it changed its title to the Yorkshire Penny Bank, a non-profit-making savings bank that had branches across Yorkshire. In order to encourage the habit of saving from an early age, the Yorkshire Penny Bank opened the world's first school bank in 1865. He also tried to make life easier for small businesses by introducing cheque books for them to use in 1872. In 1959 it changed its name to Yorkshire Bank Limited, having been able to offer overdrafts since 1911, when it became a limited liability company.

During the miners' strike in the 1980s, it offered miners who had a mortgage with them a deferment, allowing them to postpone payments for the duration of the dispute – so it was still maintaining its founder's philanthropic principals 130 years later.

Bits and Pieces

During my research I came across several interesting facts that didn't justify an article of their own, but which I wanted to share. Here follows a few.

Our Town Hall was designed by the same architect who designed the Houses of Parliament. When Piece Hall was built in 1779 it was in a field on the edge of town. With falling use for its original purpose after being sold to Halifax Corporation in 1868, it was turned into a wholesale fruit and veg market. Shibden Hall first belonged to the Otes family, then the Savile and Waterhouse families before it was owned by the Listers. There are eleven blue plaques around Halifax: ten celebrating distinguished people and one celebrating the formation of Halifax AFC. The cement used to build the Palace Theatre and Hippodrome in 1903 had sugar added to it to prevent it from freezing during very cold weather. The theatre closed in 1959 and was demolished. The first North Bridge was opened in 1774 and built of stone. The present bridge was completed in 1871. There are two- and three-storey houses and a couple of streets on top of Halifax market's outer walls. They were originally meant for market traders and managers. Their water supply was a well near the Market Street entrance.

Above left: Our magnificent Town Hall.

Above right: Our Town Hall's beauty is probably underrated by us.

Below left: South Gate, Piece Hall.

Below right: Not a vegetable stall in sight these days.

Houses above Borough Market.

C

Calder (River)

High on the moors above Todmorden, 764 feet above it on Heald Moor to be precise, the River Calder has its source. It then meanders through various Calderdale towns until it reaches the southern boundaries of Halifax. It doesn't pass through the town – it leaves that privilege to its tributary, the Hebble Brook. The Calder carries on through Elland and Brighouse until it reaches Castleford where it joins the River Aire.

Its name means either 'hard or violent water' or 'river of stones'. Judging by its appearance as it flows through the village where I live, some local primary school children and I opted for the latter. There are a further seven rivers called Calder;

Why the River Calder is a 'river of stones'.

three are in Australia, one in Cumbria and two in Scotland (where a further four tributaries of the River Clyde also carry the name Calder, or variations of it).

Once fishermen would have stood a good chance of catching salmon in it. Sadly this has not been the case for many years. Thanks to pollution, the last of these fish was pulled out of the river in 1850 – and that was downriver at Wakefield. Due to the geology of the moorland area where some of the upland streams that feed into the Calder begin their journeys, the water is too acidic to support many fish. However, things have gradually improved and some of them have a variety of coarse fish stock, which then find their way into the Calder.

Despite all the pollution the Industrial Revolution threw at it, today the river feeds thirty-nine reservoirs along its length.

Flooding has caused problems over many centuries, with the first recorded incident destroying Elland Bridge in 1615. The record of 1775 described the flood level as being 'the highest ever' – until then. But modern residents of many towns and villages along the Calder would have disagreed with that assessment, as at Christmas 2015 60 mm of rain fell in just twenty-four hours. The Calder overflowed its banks and caused chaos in numerous households. Since that 1775 pronouncement there have been over ninety occasions when the Calder or its tributaries have flooded.

The Calder at Copley Village.

Canopy of Smoke – Why Wainhouse Tower Was Built

Long before Calderdale Council started considering their Air Quality Action Plan, or John Wainhouse even thought about building his chimney that turned into a tower, people were concerned about the quality of the air we breathe and what could be done to make it cleaner. You can trace the anxiety back as far as 1273 when the use of coal was prohibited in London. Even then it was considered to be harmful to people's health. Not that London learned its lesson. I remember as an eight-year-old child in that city trying to find my way to school in fog so thick I had to feel my way along the walls of houses. It was called 'smog' to illustrate the combination of smoke and fog and it happened in Halifax too, thanks to all the mills spewing out smoke. The geography of the town didn't help any more then than it does now. Stand on one of the hills above the town and you can be in brilliant sunshine, while the valley below can be misty and overcast. That may well have been why the tenters were up on hilltops – they needed the sunshine to bleach their cloth.

Wainhouse Tower rising above the 'canopy of smoke'. (Tom Threlfall)

Above: Wainhouse Tower is a much loved Halifax folly. (Tom Threlfall)

Below: Wainhouse Tower (centre of horizon) can be seen from all over Halifax. (Tom Threlfall)

The Smoke Abatement Act of 1870 prompted John Wainhouse to build a chimney the following year. He owned the dye works in Washer Lane and was concerned about the contribution his factory was making to the dreadful air pollution in Halifax. It was so bad that in 1837 Anne Lister described her home town as 'a large smoke-canopied commercial town'. So the problem had been recognised long before anything was done about it. Wainhouse intended to create a better draught and so carry smoke up and away from the valley and, incidentally, his home (now the Wainhouse Tavern). Before the chimney was completed, Wainhouse sold his Washer Lane factory and the chimney became redundant. So Wainhouse decided to change the purpose of the part-built structure and simultaneously irritate his neighbour, Sir Henry Edwards. Sir Henry had been annoying him with various threats of summonses, so why not get his revenge?

Sir Henry cherished the privacy he enjoyed at his Pye Nest home and boasted that even when he was strolling round his grounds he could not be seen. Wainhouse thought it would be fun to invade that privacy. He decided to build the chimney higher and turn it into a folly that the public could visit. It took more than three years to complete at a cost of £15,000 by the time it was finished in 1875. That would be over a million pounds in today's money. And was it worth it, did Wainhouse achieve his objective? Yes indeed! Wainhouse Tower is around 253 feet high and the Victorian public could climb its 403 steps to the top. There they could not only gaze into Sir Henry's grounds

Wainhouse Tower window feature. (Tom Threlfall)

but also see for miles in all directions. You still can, if you've got the energy. It is open on bank holidays, between 11 a.m. and 4 p.m. (last ascent 3.30 p.m.), and the entry fee is £3 for adults with concessions for children. A family ticket for two adults and two children is £10 at the time of writing (2019).

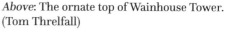

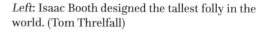

Above: The ornate top of Wainhouse Tower. (Tom Threlfall)

Left: Isaac Booth designed the tallest folly in the world. (Tom Threlfall)

D

Diamonds

Halifax isn't usually associated with cutting and polishing diamonds, but for a while, during the Second World War, it was. The story of how an engineering firm in Halifax came to play a vital role in Britain's war effort started on Whitsun weekend 1940. That was when Germany showed that the 'phoney war' was over by invading Belgium and the Netherlands, and when Churchill gave his famous 'blood, sweat and tears' speech.

Industrial diamonds are not of a good enough quality to be used as gems. In fact, 70 per cent of all diamonds mined are classed as 'industrial' and are used for purposes like cutting, drilling, polishing and grinding where other minerals are not hard enough. They may not be as beautiful as their gem-quality sisters, but they are extremely valuable in a different way.

Uncut industrial diamond. (Courtesy of Shieldforyoureyes under Creative Commons 2.0)

Both Germany and the Allies needed industrial diamonds in the manufacture of aircraft parts and armaments, so two separate and unrelated raids were planned to remove the stocks that were kept in Amsterdam before the Nazis could get their hands on them.

One raid was carried out by one military man and two civilian diamond experts. That raid had all the ingredients of a Hollywood thriller, except that it actually happened. The British government felt it was imperative that the diamonds should be held safely in London and so lent the three men the W-class destroyer HMS *Walpole* (which had been launched in February 1918), their other destroyers being needed for more urgent duties. This ship took them to Holland and back on Whit Monday 1940. One of the experts was Jan Smit, whose name appears again later on. His father was the head of J. K. Smit & Zonen, a long-established diamond dealership in Amsterdam. He persuaded the heads of other important diamond companies to entrust their stock to the three men to be taken to London for safe-keeping. The two experts also tried to get into the Amsterdamsche Bank with the intention of blowing open the time-locked vault to get to the diamond stocks kept there too, but it was locked over the Whitsun weekend and they could not get in. So they just took the diamonds they had been given already and got them safely back to London. All this happened in just one day. A promise was made that all the companies would get their diamonds back after the war. This promise was kept.

The second raid was carried out by a lone MI6 agent, Lieutenant Colonel M. R. Chidson, based in The Hague in Holland and was equally as exciting. He had long been expecting the German invasion, although the Dutch thought their neutrality would protect them. He had prepared himself well to get into the Amsterdam Mart, where there was a very large cache of diamonds. However, it took him twenty-four hours to get the vault open, which he did just as German troops made their way in with the same intention – to take possession of the diamonds. Luckily he got away and managed to get his haul to Queen Wilhelmina, who was then whisked off to safety in England with her family and the Dutch government.

There was no point in rescuing the diamonds only for them to sit doing nothing in London. They needed to be put to work helping Britain win the war. But before they could do that, they had to be cut and polished. There were very few craftsmen in the country qualified to do the job which, under normal circumstances, would require an apprenticeship of five or six years.

This is where William Asquith Ltd of Halifax came into the picture. This major machine tool manufacturing company had built up a formidable reputation during the course of its then seventy-five-year existence. The company's sales operations were run from offices in London by Bob Asquith, who heard about the problem and boasted that his company could design machines capable of doing what was required to bring the rough diamonds to a useable standard. The government was desperate and took the firm up on its claim.

First, the design team needed to know what was required and to this end an expert, the same Jan Smit mentioned earlier, was brought in for a few weeks to explain the pitfalls involved and demonstrate how he would get a stone from its initial rough state to the quality needed for the end product. In his booklet explaining the whole story of how Asquith's design team achieved this through their specially designed machines, Leslie Harkness says, 'The aim of polishing is always the same – to finish with the highest yield by weight whilst positioning the final gem inside the crystal with any flaws away from critical areas in which they would repeat several times when viewed through the top surface...'

It is worth noting that Mr Harkness was a twenty-year-old employee with the company when all this began, but wrote his very detailed booklet in his late eighties. It was a remarkable achievement and a fascinating read. He explains in detail and with many illustrations not only facts about diamond shapes, cuts and facets, but how these were traditionally achieved. I imagine the design team would have had to understand all that in order to work out how to produce machines that could bring about the same ends.

Despite a number of setbacks, the team did indeed develop machines that enabled the rough stones to be honed to work-perfect in six weeks. The system worked successfully for seven years, the machines being purchased post-war by De Beers for use in their Johannesburg premises.

I have not been able to find proof, but as the merchants got their diamonds back after the war, I have to wonder whether the Halifax diamonds were those 'rescued' by Lieutenant Colonel Chidson and given to Queen Wilhelmina, and if she donated them to the British government in gratitude for the sanctuary we had afforded her and her government.

Equator

Halifax was described as being 'geographically remote' until the sixteenth century by the historian and author Dr John A. Hargreaves in his book *Halifax*. But over 200 million years ago it was even more remote. It would have been located south of the equator, roughly where South Africa is now. But continental drift gradually shifted us to our more familiar location.

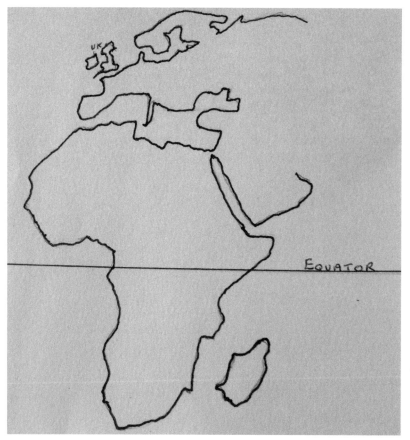

We were much, much further south at one time. (Bob Wood)

F

Film and TV Locations

The Halifax area has provided locations and ideas for many films, the first probably being *Helen of Four Gates*, produced in 1920 and filmed at Hebden Bridge.

Alan Bennett wrote his first play for television in 1969, which was broadcast by the BBC in 1972. It was about a Halifax cycling club's trip to Fountains Abbey and was called *A Day Out*.

There have also been some TV series filmed, at least in part, in Halifax. Some scenes in the 2008 crime series Red Riding were filmed in the town. It was a three-part television adaptation of a trilogy of novels by West Yorkshire-born author David Peace about police corruption and organised crime. There was also *Last Tango in Halifax* and *Happy Valley*. Both had scenes filmed in Halifax including some at Princess Building, Saddleworth Road, King Cross Road, West View Park in Warley, a café in Market Arcade and another café in Crossley Street.

Shibden Hall where *Gentleman Jack* was filmed. (Tom Threlfall)

The most recent television series to be filmed in our area was the highly successful *Gentleman Jack* about Anne Lister. This was written by Sally Wainwright who grew up just down the road from Halifax, in Sowerby Bridge. She also wrote two of the series already mentioned, *Last Tango in Halifax* and *Happy Valley*. Much of *Gentleman Jack* was filmed in and around Shibden Hall itself; so actual incidents gleaned from Sally reading Anne Lister's coded diaries for herself were filmed where they had actually taken place in Lister's lifetime. Many other Yorkshire locations beyond Halifax itself were also used.

Halifax has provided a number of locations for award-winning films too. These include *Room At The Top*, which heralded the start of the realist genre of films known as 'Kitchen Sink' dramas in 1959. The Clarence Hotel on Lister Lane and the Town Hall appeared in this film. *This Sporting Life* in 1963 was seen more as a 'British New Wave' film, rather than 'Kitchen Sink'. Part of it was filmed at the Halifax stadium Thrum Hall; it starred the late Richard Harris who was nominated for an Oscar for Best Actor in a Leading Role, but he lost out to Sidney Poitier that year. The Piece Hall featured in the 1996 film *Brassed Off* as the location for the brass band competition heats.

For Valour – Victoria Cross Recipients Connected to Halifax

The Victoria Cross (VC) is the highest decoration of the United Kingdom honours system. It is awarded for gallantry 'in the face of the enemy' to members of the British armed services. The VC can be awarded to civilians if they are 'serving with the armed forces'. To date only five have been bestowed on civilians (four in the Indian Rebellion of 1857–58 and one in Afghanistan in 1879).

Before the VC, the highest award for gallantry was the Order of the Bath, but it could only be given to senior officers. To balance things out a bit, the Distinguished Conduct Medal was created in 1854 for NCOs and privates.

Other countries had medals for gallantry regardless of rank. The idea that Britain should have one too came from Liberal MP and former naval officer Captain Thomas Scobell in December 1854 and the Duke of Newcastle, the then Secretary of State for War who, in January 1855 announced the creation of a new medal for 'a signal act of valour in the presence of the enemy'.

Both Queen Victoria and Prince Albert were actively involved in the decoration's establishment. Indeed, it was Prince Albert who changed the name of the medal from the Military Order of Victoria to the Victoria Cross.

The queen took particular interest in the design of the medal and suggested reducing its size slightly from that shown in the original design. She also changed the slogan on the front of the medal. Originally it was 'For the Brave', but she felt that implied that anyone who was not awarded the VC was not brave; consequently, she changed it to 'For Valour'. In addition, she changed the medal material from copper to bronze.

Victoria also made it clear that she wished to personally present as many of the medals as possible and chose 26 June 1857 to do so for the first time. She also decided to stay on horseback while she performed the ceremony for the first sixty-two recipients of the new medal. At the time of writing 1,358 VCs have been awarded, three of them being awarded twice to the same men.

Few of the men in the following list of VC winners were born in Halifax, but there is a connection to the town in some way or another for each of them. I have listed them in alphabetical order, but it is worth noting that nine of the VCs served with the Duke of Wellington's Regiment (West Riding). I have also mentioned when a medal is on display in the Duke of Wellington's Regimental Museum within the Bankfield Museum.

Private James Bergin VC, 33rd Regiment of Foot (later the Duke of Wellington's Regiment)

Bergin was awarded his VC for the same action as Drummer Michael Magner, which took place on 13 April 1866 in Abyssinia during the assault of Magdala. Their citation reads:

> Lieutenant-General Lord Napier reports that, whilst the head of the column of attack was checked by the obstacles at the gate, a small stream of Officers and men of the 33rd Regiment and an Officer of Engineers, breaking away from the main approach to Magdala, and climbing up a cliff, reached the defences, and forced their way over the wall, and through the strong and thorny fence, thus turning the defenders of the gateway. The first two men to enter, and the first in Magdala, were Drummer Magner and Private Bergin, of the 33rd Regiment.

Bergin was Irish by birth and died in Poona, India, aged thirty-five. His medals are held by the Duke of Wellington's Regimental Museum in Bankfield Museum.

Private Richard Burton VC, 1st Battalion, the Duke of Wellington's Regiment (West Riding)

Private Burton was another soldier who was born and died beyond the borders of Halifax, being born in Leicestershire and died in Scotland. But, like Private Bergin, he served with 'The Dukes'. His long citation reads:

> In Italy on 8th October, 1944, two Companies of the Duke of Wellington's Regiment moved forward to take a strongly held feature 760 metres high. Recapture of this

feature was vital at this stage of the operation as it dominated all the ground on the main axis of advance.

The assaulting troops made good progress to within 20 yards of the crest when they came. under withering fire from Spandaus on the crest. The leading platoon was held up and the Platoon Commander was wounded. The Company Commander took another platoon, of which Private Burton was runner, through to assault the crest from which four Spandaus at least were firing. Private Burton rushed forward and, engaging the first Spandau position with his Tommy gun, killed the crew of three. When the assault was again held up by murderous fire from two more machine guns Private Burton, again showing complete disregard for his own safety, dashed forward toward the first machine gun using his Tommy gun until his ammunition was exhausted. He then picked up a Bren gun and firing from the hip succeeded in killing or wounding the crews of the two machine guns. Thanks to his outstanding courage the Company was then able to consolidate on the forward slope of the feature.

The enemy immediately counter-attacked fiercely but Private Burton, in spite of most of his comrades being either dead or wounded, once again dashed forward on his own initiative and directed such accurate fire with his Bren gun on the enemy that they retired leaving the feature firmly in our hands.

The enemy later counter-attacked again on the adjoining platoon position and Private Burton, who had placed himself on the flank, brought such accurate fire to bear that this counter-attack also failed to dislodge the Company from its position.

Private Burton's magnificent gallantry and total disregard of his own safety during many hours of fierce fighting in mud and continuous rain were an inspiration to all his comrades.

Sergeant James Firth VC, 1st Battalion, the Duke of Wellington's Regiment (West Riding)

Sergeant Firth was from Sheffield, which is where he died. He lost an eye during the action that is recounted in his citation and wore an eye patch for the rest of his life. He won his VC during the Boer War in South Africa and his citation reads:

During the action at Plewton's Farm, near Arundel, Cape Colony, on the 24th February, 1900. Lance Corporal Blackman having been wounded and lying exposed to a hot fire at a range of 400–500 yards, Sergeant Firth picked him up and carried him to cover. Later in the day, when the enemy had advanced to within a short distance of the firing line, Second Lieutenant Wilson being dangerously wounded and in a most exposed position, Sergeant Firth carried him over the ridge, which was being held by the troops, to shelter and was himself shot through the nose and eye whilst doing so.

Private Joel Holmes VC

Joel Holmes was born at Great Gomersal in 1821 and is buried in All Souls cemetery in Boothtown. He served with the 84th Regiment of Foot (later the York and Lancaster Regiment) and was posted to India with his regiment in 1857 during the Indian Mutiny. He won his VC in the same year for action at Charbagh Bridge and his officer mentioned that five men had been killed in as many seconds at the gun they were manning. He mentioned that Private Holmes was the first to volunteer to man the gun in their place. His citation reads: 'For distinguished conduct in volunteering to assist in working a gun of Captain Maude's Battery, under heavy fire, from which gun nearly all the artillerymen had been shot away.'

2nd Lieutenant James Palmer Huffam VC, 5th Battalion, the Duke of Wellington's Regiment (West Riding)

James Palmer Huffam was born in Scotland and died in Middlesex. His citation reads:

> For conspicuous bravery and devotion to duty on 31st August, 1918. With three men he rushed an enemy machine-gun post and put it out of action. His post was then heavily attacked and he withdrew fighting, carrying a wounded comrade. Again on the night of the 31st August, 1918, at St Servin's Farm, accompanied by two men only, he rushed an enemy machine-gun post, capturing eight prisoners and enabling the advance to continue. Throughout the whole of the fighting from 29th August to 1st September 1918 he showed the utmost gallantry.

He started his army career as an eighteen-year-old private in 1915 in a different regiment. After promotion to sergeant he was recommended for a commission, which he got at the age of twenty. It was then that he joined The Dukes.

2nd Lieutenant Henry Kelly VC, 10th Battalion, the Duke of Wellington's Regiment (West Riding)

Henry Kelly was born in Manchester and died in Prestwich at the age of ninety-three. His citation reads:

> For most conspicuous bravery in attack at Le Sars on 4th October, 1916. He twice rallied his company under the heaviest fire and finally led the only three available men into the enemy trench and there remained bombing until two of them had become casualties and enemy reinforcements had arrived. He then carried his

Company Sergeant Major, who had been wounded, back to our trenches, a distance of 70 yards, and subsequently three other soldiers. He set a fine example of gallantry and endurance.

He also fought in the International Brigade in the Spanish Civil War from 1936 to 1938. Later he fought in the Second World War too. His VC is held by the Duke of Wellington's Regiment museum at Bankfield Museum.

Private Arnold Loosemore VC, 8th Battalion, the Duke of Wellington's Regiment (West Riding)

Born and died in Sheffield, his citation reads:

For most conspicuous bravery and initiative during the attack on a strongly held enemy position south of Langemarck, Flanders on 11th August, 1917. His platoon having been checked by heavy machine-gun fire, he crawled through partially-cut wire, dragging his Lewis gun with him, and singled handed dealt with a strong part of the enemy killing about twenty of them and thus covering the consolidation of the position taken up by his platoon. Immediately afterwards his Lewis gun was blown up by a bomb and three of the enemy rushed for him, but he shot them all with his revolver. Later, he shot several enemy snipers, exposing himself to heavy fire each time. On returning to the original post he also brought back a wounded comrade under heavy fire at the risk of his life. He displayed throughout an utter disregard of danger.

Sadly, the following year he was shot in the left leg, which had to be amputated. He died of tuberculosis, having spent the last year of his life confined to bed.

Private John Pearson VC

Although John Pearson was born in Leeds and died in Canada, he served with the 8th Regiment of Light Dragoons (Hussars). They formed part of the Light Brigade, which fought in the Crimean War and took part in the famous Charge of the Light Brigade immortalised in Tennyson's poem of the same name. He also served in India during the Mutiny where he was wounded by a sword-cut to his right shoulder during action at Gwalior. Following this action, it was decided that four Victoria Crosses should be awarded to the regiment and after a ballot had been taken four men were chosen to receive the honour. Pearson was one of them. The citation reads:

Selected for the Victoria Cross by their companions. In the gallant charge made by a Squadron of the Regiment at Gwalior, on the 17th June, 1858, when supported by a division of the Bombay Horse Artillery, and Her Majesty's 95th Regiment, they routed the enemy, who were advancing against Brigadier Smith's position, charged through the rebel camp into two batteries, capturing and bringing into their camp two of the enemy's guns, under a heavy and converging fire from the fort and town.

For a while he lived here in various parts of Halifax, where his youngest three children were born.

Temporary Acting Leading Seaman James Joseph Magennis

Born in Belfast, James Magennis returned there after the war but later lived in Bradford. However, he died in Halifax Infirmary in 1986, so I have included him here among our heroes. His citation reads:

Leading Seaman Magennis served as Diver in His Majesty's Midget Submarine XE-3 for her attack on 31st July, 1945, on a Japanese cruiser of the Atago class. Owing to the fact that XE-3 was tightly jammed under the target the diver's hatch could not be fully opened, and Magennis had to squeeze himself through the narrow space available. He experienced great difficulty in placing his limpets on the bottom of the cruiser owing both to the foul state of the bottom and to the pronounced slope upon which the limpets would not hold. Before a limpet could be placed therefore Magennis had thoroughly to scrape the area clear of barnacles, and in order to secure the limpets he had to tie them in pairs by a line passing under the cruiser keel. This was very tiring work for a diver, and he was moreover handicapped by a steady leakage of oxygen which was ascending in bubbles to the surface. A lesser man would have been content to place a few limpets and then to return to the craft. Magennis, however, persisted until he had placed his full outfit before returning to the craft in an exhausted condition. Shortly after withdrawing Lieutenant Fraser endeavoured to jettison his limpet carriers, but one of these would not release itself and fall clear of the craft. Despite his exhaustion, his oxygen leak and the fact that there was every probability of his being sighted, Magennis at once volunteered to leave the craft and free the carrier rather than allow a less experienced diver to undertake the job. After seven minutes of nerve-racking work he succeeded in releasing the carrier. Magennis displayed very great courage and devotion to duty and complete disregard for his own safety.

Private Arthur Poulter VC, 1/4 of Battalion, the Duke of Wellington's Regiment (West Riding)

Born in North Yorkshire, Private Poulter initially joined the West Riding Regiment in 1916, transferring to The Dukes in 1918. It was while serving with them that he won his VC. His citation reads:

> For most conspicuous bravery when acting as a stretcher-bearer, at Erquinghem-Lys, on 10th April, 1918. On ten occasions Private Poulter carried badly wounded men on his back to a safe locality, through a particularly heavy artillery and machine-gun barrage. Again, after a withdrawal over the river had been ordered, Private Poulter returned in full view of the enemy, who were advancing, and carried back another man who had been left behind wounded. He bandaged-up over forty men under fire, and his conduct throughout the whole day was a magnificent example to all ranks. This very gallant soldier was seriously wounded when attempting another rescue in the face of the enemy.

What the citation doesn't say is that one by one all his company's stretcher-bearers were killed or wounded. The enemy was firing at them from only 50–100 yards away and on the first day alone Poulter went out ten times to carry the wounded back to safety – a distance of 400 to 500 hundred yards across a river bridge to where the field hospital was. His medal is in The Duke's museum at Bankfield Museum.

Private Henry Tandey VC, 5th Battalion, the Duke of Wellington's Regiment (West Riding)

Henry Tandey was born in Leamington Spa and died in Coventry aged eighty-six. His citation reads:

> For most conspicuous bravery and initiative during the capture of the village and the crossings at Marcoing and the subsequent counter-attack on 28th September, 1918. When, during the advance on Marcoing, his platoon was held by machine-gun fire, he at once crawled forward, located the machine-gun, and with his Lewis gun team knocked it out. On arrival at the crossing he restored the plank bridge under a hail of bullets, thus enabling the first crossing to be made at this vital spot. Later in the evening, during an attack, he, with eight comrades, was surrounded by an overwhelming number of Germans and, though the position was apparently helpless, he led a bayonet charge through them, fighting so fiercely that 37 of the enemy were driven into the hands of the

remainder of his company. Although twice wounded he refused to leave until the fight was won.

He initially joined the Green Howards, transferring later to The Dukes. He won the three highest awards for bravery in the space of six weeks! These were the Distinguished Conduct Medal, the Military Medal and bar, and then the Victoria Cross.

Corporal (Acting Sergeant) Hanson Victor Turner VC, West Yorkshire Regiment (the Prince of Wales's Own) – originally served with The Dukes

This soldier was born in Hampshire but lived in Copley and, like his father before him, joined The Dukes. He then transferred to the Prince of Wales's Own. His citation reads:

> In Burma, at Ningthoukong on the night of 6th–7th June, 1944, an attack was made by Japanese with medium and light machine guns. The attack largely fell on the position held by a platoon of which Sergeant Turner was one of the Section Commanders. The enemy were able to use grenades with deadly effect. Three machine-guns in the platoon were destroyed and the platoon was forced to give ground. Sergeant Turner with coolness and fine leadership reorganised his party and with a doggedness and spirit of endurance of the highest order repelled all attacks. The position was held throughout the night. When it was clear that the Japanese were attempting to outflank the position, Sergeant Turner, armed with grenades, boldly and fearlessly attacked them single handed. He went back five times for more grenades; and on the sixth occasion, still singlehanded, he was killed while throwing a grenade among the enemy.
>
> His conduct on that night will ever be remembered by the Regiment. His superb leadership and undaunted will to win in the early stages of the attack was undoubtedly instrumental in preventing the enemy plan from succeeding. The number of enemy found dead the next morning was ample evidence of the effect his grenade throwing had had.
>
> He displayed outstanding valour and had not the slightest thought of his own safety. He died on the battlefield in a spirit of supreme self-sacrifice.

His body was recovered and all the official records show him as being buried in the Imphal War Cemetery in India. His name appears on the war memorial outside St Stephen's Church in Copley. His VC was bought by Halifax Town Council and is in The Duke's museum at Bankfield Museum.

Above: War memorial at St Stephen's Church, Copley.

Below: St Stephen's Church, Copley. (Tom Threlfall)

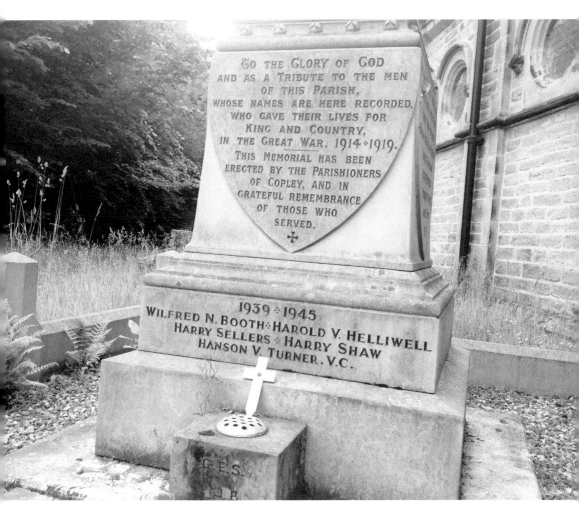

Hanson Turner VC remembered.

Gibbet

There's a gruesome reminder in Bankfield Museum of just how severely Halifax punished thieves and other criminals in the past. They were beheaded by the gibbet, and the blade that chopped so many heads off is held in the museum. There's a replica gibbet to be seen now, at the junction of Bedford Street North and the appropriately named Gibbet Street. Thankfully the gibbet doesn't work now!

It seems that other countries rather liked the idea of disposing of their criminal fraternity in this manner (and their aristocrats, in the case of France) and built their own forms of the automated axe. It may have gone by different names, but the idea was the same. One of its early admirers was James Morton, the 4th Earl of Morton and Regent of Scotland, who spotted it when he was in Halifax. His regency entailed acting

Off with his head! (Tom Threlfall)

on behalf of the child who would later unite England and Scotland by succeeding to the throne when Elizabeth I died. He became known to us as James I, but he was James VI to his Scottish subjects and to James Morton. The earl had a similar contraption built and used in Edinburgh, where it was nicknamed 'The Maiden'. Ironically, he lost his own head on it when he was executed for his part in the murder of Mary Queen of Scots' first husband, Lord Darnley.

In Germany they had a device that was known as the Fallbeil ('falling axe') where it was used in various regions from around the nineteenth century. A later version executed over 16,000 prisoners between 1933 and 1945. Similar contraptions were also used in the eighteenth and nineteenth centuries in Belgium and as late as the twentieth century in Greece, Sweden and Switzerland. The French had sixteen names for their guillotine; my personal favourite is Le Prix Goncourt des Assassins (The Goncourt Prize for Murderers).

Meanwhile, the Halifax gibbet was first recorded as doing its grisly job as early as 1286; John of Dalton was the person who lost his head on that occasion. This method of execution was considered much more humane than hacking a head off with an axe or sword. But was it? When the French were busy executing their gentry as fast as they could, the question arose as to how long the brain in a severed head actually retained consciousness. A Dr Beaurieux decided to watch an execution and see if he could detect any sign of life in the head afterwards. As he appeared to get a response when he called the dead man's name, he reached the conclusion that there was still some consciousness for quite a few seconds after the head had parted company with the body.

Forerunner of the French guillotine. (Tom Threlfall)

Have a Drink on Me – Some
Interesting Pubs

There are plenty of pubs to visit in Halifax and nearby, but I have chosen to highlight five that are a bit different in some way or have an interesting history or connections.

Cheers!

A favourite meeting place for Chartists.

The Union Cross Hotel, Nos 10–12 Old Market, Halifax

The oldest pub in town and a Grade II listed building, it has been serving customers since at least 1535, when its clientele were travellers using packhorses and coaches. It was originally known as the Crosse Inn. John Wesley tried to preach from the hostelry's steps, but failed to capture his audience. Daniel Defoe, the author of *Robinson Crusoe* is reputed to have stayed there.

Dog & Partridge, Sowood

This is a country pub that holds a Christmas party in February and has a history that can be traced back to the Elizabethan period.

Standard of Freedom, Skircoat Green

The pub's original name was The Waggoners. Chartism in the town is mentioned elsewhere, but the Standard of Freedom Inn has a connection to its development. When supporters of the movement gathered there in strength, its landlord was said to have announced, 'The people of Skircoat Green shall join in that march of freedom. I will raise the standard of freedom at this inn.'

White Swan Hotel, Princess Street, Halifax

The present building is Victorian, but both its name and the name of the street it stands on have changed since it was known as the White Swan Inn & Posting House in 1585. Back then it was on Crown Street and was a coaching inn for services to Leeds, London, Manchester and Liverpool. That building was demolished in 1858 when Princess Street was constructed. The 'new' hotel opened in 1858.

The Fleece Inn, Westgate, Elland

Now surrounded by modern flats and houses, this early seventeenth-century building was originally a farmhouse before it was converted into an inn. A man being chased for cheating during a business deal took refuge here, but was caught and murdered in the early nineteenth century; he left his bloody handprint on the stairs. All efforts to remove it failed and eventually that part of the staircase was burned in the 1970s. The pub and its surroundings are known for ghostly apparitions, who still put in an appearance from time to time.

Above: The Fleece Inn is now surrounded by modern housing.

Left: Old beam in the bar of The Fleece Inn.

I

In Hot Water – Lilly Lane Baths

Spa treatments have been popular, to varying degrees, since Roman times and reached the height of their popularity in the nineteenth and early twentieth centuries in Britain. A Halifax plumber got in on the trend somewhat earlier though and built some spa baths.

In 1784 Thomas Rawlinson had the foresight to take out a lease on land at Coldwell Ing owned by the Waterhouse Charities. He then built a beautiful red-brick building with hot, cold, tepid and sulphur baths available inside, together with a dining room and changing rooms. The substantial grounds outside offered a variety of diversions,

Bath Street. (Paul Hadfield)

including a lovely outdoor swimming pool, beautiful gardens to stroll in and various other diversions such as bowling greens and quoits to keep clients occupied when not using the indoor facilities. It was conveniently located near the Hebble Brook and was supplied with water from springs onsite at Coldwell Ing and Greece Field (where the railway station is now).

At 1 guinea (£1 1s – worth around £126 today) a year, membership and use of the baths was beyond the reach of most ordinary people at that time. However, Branwell Brontë was one of its distinguished visitors, so it seems he could manage the membership fee.

The baths were located at Lilly Lane, which had been named after Edward Lilley, who ran a fulling mill on the site in the early years of the seventeenth century. These days the lane is only a few yards long before it reaches a footbridge over the railway. There's no sign of the baths now, as Rawlinson sold the site to the railways, so all you can see now are railway lines.

Bridge over railway at the bottom of this shortened road. (Paul Hadfield)

J

John Christie

Halifax has more than its fair share of heroes, but its most infamous son must surely be the serial killer John Christie, who murdered at least six women including his wife. Born in Northowram in 1899, he was hanged for murder at Pentonville Prison, London, on 15 July 1953, at the age of fifty-four.

Christie left Northowram to join the army in 1916, aged seventeen and a half. A few months before the First World War ended he was sent to France where he suffered in a mustard gas attack. For the next three and a half years he was unable to speak; he put it down to the effect of the mustard gas, but there are those who think that he was faking it to get sympathy.

He married Ethel Simpson in May 1920 and they lived together in Sheffield, but the marriage was not a happy one. His life of crime started at this time. He began working at the post office, but the job came to an end when he was accused of stealing hundreds of pounds worth of postal orders. He was tried and sentenced to three months in prison. He then moved to London, after a short spell in Manchester where

John Christie's home village.

he worked as a painter, leaving Ethel behind in Sheffield. He joined the Royal Air Force in 1924 after he moved to London, but was discharged after serving only a few months.

He roamed around London, living in various places for the next nine years and again engaged in a life of mostly petty crime. However, it was during this period that he was jailed for six months for grievous bodily harm and later for theft of a car, which resulted in a further three months in prison.

Even before his marriage to Ethel he had consorted with prostitutes to satisfy his urges for violent sex. These visits continued even after he and Ethel were reconciled and she joined him in London.

Then he got a strange job, considering his criminal past: he applied to join the police in 1936 and was accepted! He only resigned in 1943, by which time he had committed his first murder. Ruth Fuerst, a part-time prostitute, was his first victim – as far as we know – and he buried her in the garden.

After his resignation from the police he worked as a clerk at a radio factory and murdered his second victim, Muriel Eady, in 1944. She joined Ruth in the garden.

He waited until November 1949 before murdering again. This time the victim was his upstairs neighbour's wife. That neighbour was Timothy Evans, who was wrongly hanged for killing his wife Beryl, when she was actually one of Christie's victims, Christie having appeared as a star witness at his trial. (In 1966 Evans received a posthumous royal pardon.) During Timothy Evans' trial Christie's past criminal record was mentioned and this caused him to lose his job at the Post Office Savings Bank. But he next found work with British Road Transport services as a clerk, which he suddenly resigned from in December 1952. Perhaps the fact that he had killed his wife and hidden her under the front room floorboards had unsettled him. But not too much, because the next month he killed another prostitute – Kathleen Maloney. The month after that it was the turn of a young lady who had visited him with her boyfriend. She was Hectorina MacLennan, who made the mistake of going back to his flat on her own later on.

His last three victims were all hidden in an alcove behind a cupboard in his kitchen. Obviously, the place began to smell, with all these bodies rotting away in there. He used copious amounts of disinfectant around the place to try to disguise it.

The end came later in March 1953, the month when he killed his last victim, and in a way it was his own fault that he got caught. He decided to illegally sublet his flat to a couple, keeping their rent money for himself. When the real landlord found out he evicted the couple, but allowed another of the tenants in the house to use Christie's kitchen. That tenant discovered the bodies of the three women in the hidden alcove.

Christie went on the run, but was picked up by the police. He was tried in July 1953, found guilty and sentenced to be hanged. There was a bit of real gallows humour right at the end of his life when Christie allegedly complained to the executioner, Albert Pierrepoint, that his nose was itchy. Pierrepoint is said to have replied, 'It won't bother you for long.'

Above: The Old Bailey –
where Christie was tried.
(Courtesy of Tony Hisgett under
Creative Commons 2.0)

Right: The Scales of Justice at
the Central Criminal Court.
(Courtesy of Tony Hisgett under
Creative Commons 2.0)

Kaylied But Safe – Halifax Street Angels

You go out for a good time on a Friday or Saturday night, but find yourself incapacitated when the evening is over. Maybe your drink was spiked, or you simply drank far too much. Perhaps your phone has run out of charge, so you can't call for a taxi or for someone to come and collect you. Have those gorgeous high heels that went perfectly with your outfit proved disastrous for your feet and the blisters they've caused make walking incredibly painful? 'If you have a problem, if no one else can help, and if you can find them, maybe you can hire … The A-Team.' In this case, the A-Team refers to the Halifax Street Angels and they find you, you don't have to go searching for them (nor are they for hire!). Launched in 2005, the Halifax Street Angels consist of volunteers who patrol the streets of central Halifax and Sowerby Bridge on Friday and Saturday nights, offering help where it is needed.

Worried about the level of violent crime on the streets around the town centre and its effect on the vulnerable in our community, a group of volunteers decided to see what they could do to help people who needed it after a night out. They started by opening a café and called for more volunteers to join them. They were overwhelmed with offers of help.

Initially run for a six-week period to see how things went. The idea was so successful it is still running at the time of writing (2019). Volunteers are out from 10 p.m. to 4 a.m., no matter what the weather flings at them, keeping an eye open for those who need assistance of some kind.

As well as meeting the needs of those on the streets, this Christian charity also runs a community café and bookshop in Halifax where people can receive advice or simply have someone unjudgmental to listen to them. They work in schools, colleges and youth groups to educate young people about the dangers of alcohol and drugs, as well as advising them on crime awareness. They also provide stewards for local community events.

And is it all worth it? The facts speak for themselves: a year after their group was formed, violent town centre crime had reduced by 42 per cent. That sounds like a 'yes' to me.

They are on Facebook and have a website for you to look at if you would like further information. Their café address is: Angels Rest Cafe & Christian Bookshop, No. 15 Crossley Street, Halifax, HX1 1UG.

Angels Rest Café.

Literary Links

Dr Phyllis Bentley OBE (1894–1977)

Phyllis Bentley was born, brought up and died in Halifax, although she did study in Cheltenham for an eternal degree from London University and also worked in London for a while. She attended Halifax High School for Girls (later known as Princess Mary High School for Girls). The school was subsequently demolished to make way for an extension to Calderdale College.

Phyllis Bentley knew from childhood that she wanted to write, and she did indeed grow up to be a prolific author, producing both novels and non-fiction books, as well as short stories and scripts. Her novels and short stories reflect life in West Yorkshire and her literary role models were the Brontës. Indeed, she became an acknowledged expert on the Brontës. She wrote a biography about them and gave lectures on them. Her most successful work was her 1932 novel *Inheritance*, the first book in a trilogy, which was dramatised for television in 1967 and starred John Thaw and James Bolam. She was awarded an honorary doctorate in 1949 by Leeds University and an OBE in 1970.

Emily Brontë (1818–48)

In 1838/39 Emily spent six months teaching at Miss Patchett's School for Girls, Law Hill, Southowram. In those days, anyone could set up a school and run it in one of the rooms in their house if they so wished. There was no legislation governing either education or working conditions for teachers at the time. So, according to her sister Charlotte, Emily worked from 6 a.m. to 11 p.m. with only half an hour's break.

Patrick Branwell Brontë (1817–48)

More famous for his drinking and drug addiction than his poetry, nonetheless Branwell was the first of the Brontës to see his work in print.

Branwell began writing poetry from around the age of eleven, but the first of his 250 poems to be published was 'Heaven and Earth', which appeared in the *Halifax Guardian* on 5 June 1841, followed by a further five of his subsequent poems.

He had another, less worthy, connection with Halifax. He was a regular at the Old Cock Hotel in the town centre, but failed to pay his bill there. The landlord wasn't going to let him get away with that, so he had a Summons sent to Branwell's Haworth Parsonage home.

Sir Thomas Browne (1605–82)

This English author was a man of many talents. He wrote around eight books, one of his most famous being *Religio Medici* (A Doctor's Religion) written in around 1635 – a worldwide best seller in its time. His work gave rise to lots of other religious-themed books for the next 100 years, despite the fact that he was not particularly devout himself. Indeed, trained anatomists such as him were viewed with distaste at the time because the Church taught that you should be concerned about your immortal soul. It was thought that anatomy students could not believe in the immortality of the soul because they cut up and examined bodies. Perhaps this is why the pope banned *Religio Medici*.

Although he was not a Halifax native, after taking his MD degree at Leiden University in Holland in 1633, he lived in the Shibden Valley (one source places him in Shibden Hall) in 1634 where he practiced medicine for a time and wrote his first book mentioned above. He was thirty years old at the time and went on to take a further MD degree at Oxford after leaving Shibden. He is described as 'an urbane, sophisticated and witty writer, who delights in collecting trivia and arcane information'. He was an intelligent man who had extensive scientific and cultural interests. He was also responsible for inventing quite a few words that are still in use today. Some of these are: electricity, medical, indigenous, ferocious, migrant, coma, anomalous, prairie, ascetic, carnivorous, ambidextrous – and there were others.

He didn't inherit his title, but received it late in his life when he was living in Norwich. The town's mayor was of a Parliamentarian persuasion and therefore refused the knighthood offered by Charles II during his visit there. Browne was the next most important citizen in Norwich by that time, so the king gave him the knighthood instead.

Daniel Defoe (*c.* 1660–1731)

An author best known for his book *Robinson Crusoe*, he also wrote a book about his travels, *A Tour Thro' the Whole Island of Great Britain*. This was partly based on his earlier trips as a merchant and partly on actual trips he undertook for this book. Both Halifax and the River Calder are mentioned in it. In their description of the book for their reprint, Penguin Books describe it as 'his deeply imaginative response to a brave new economic world'.

G. Bramwell Evens (1892–1943)

A Methodist minister at King Cross Methodist Chapel from 1929 to 1939, he had twenty nature books for both adults and children published between 1929 and 1944. His pseudonym was 'Romany', probably reflecting the fact that his mother was a Romani gypsy. He was also a well-known broadcaster for the BBC, being a pioneer natural history broadcaster.

Dr Frank King (1892–1958)

A prolific crime writer, Dr Frank King was born in Halifax. Like so many authors of his time, his work is largely forgotten now. However, he made one very significant contribution to the British film industry in that he wrote the script for *The Ghoul* – the first major horror film to be produced in the UK and based on his book of the same name (which he co-authored with Revd Leonard Hines, another Halifax man). Horror actor Boris Karloff – an English actor who was later to play Frankenstein – starred in *The Ghoul* in 1933, his first British film.

Judge James Pickles (1925–2010)

Best known as a circuit judge on the north-eastern circuit, this Halifax-born judge is mainly remembered for his controversial sentencing decisions and press statements, rather than his literary accomplishments. However, contentious to the end, he wrote two books defending his legal decisions and remarks, as well as *Off The Record*, described as 'a novel about a controversial judge not afraid to speak his mind, whose public suggestions transform his professional and sexual life'. He also wrote several plays, some being aired on radio, and was a member of Halifax Thespians and Halifax Authors' Circle.

Maurice Procter (1906–73)

Another prolific author who wrote twenty-six detective novels. He was born in Nelson Lancashire and became a policeman; however, at that time you couldn't serve as a policeman in your home town, so he moved to Halifax and worked in King Cross and

Halifax writers have produced numerous books.

Mixenden. He started writing novels while still in the police force, but as soon as he made a decent income from his books he retired from the police and concentrated on his writing. He must have done well, because latterly he and his wife spent part of the year in Spain and Gibraltar.

Laurence Sterne (1713–68)

This author and satirist was born in Ireland, but his family had strong Yorkshire links. When he was eleven years old he was sent to Hipperholme Grammar School under the guardianship of his Uncle Richard.

   As an adult he became a vicar and is probably best known as the author of a book whose full title is *The Life and Opinions of Tristram Shandy, Gentleman*. The title is somewhat misleading, since Tristram isn't even born for the first half of the story and has only reached the age of three by the end. However, this amusing piece of literature made Sterne famous well beyond Britain's shores.

Sally Wainwright (b. 1964)

Strictly speaking, we can't really claim this prolific writer of television dramas as one of our own as she was brought up in Sowerby Bridge. But the two towns are so close that I am including her anyway. She began her career by writing episodes for some of the soaps. Her first scripts to be seen on TV were two episodes of *Emmerdale* in 1991. She also wrote for a number of other television series, including *Coronation Street*. She then went on to write *At Home with the Braithwaites*, which she also produced. In addition, she has written for radio. She is probably best known in our area for *Last Tango in Halifax* and *Happy Valley*. At the time of writing, her latest drama was the story of Anne Lister of Shibden Hall; *Gentleman Jack* was not only a big hit here but also in the USA, resulting in a huge influx of American tourists to Halifax and a phenomenal 700-plus per cent increase in visitors to Shibden Hall.

Other writers associated with towns near Halifax include the poet Ted Hughes (born in Mytholmroyd), Margaret Thatcher's press secretary Bernard Ingham (born in Hebden Bridge) and colourful author, William Holt, a native of Todmorden. Although not from the area, American poet, novelist and short-story writer Sylvia Plath is buried in Heptonstall.

M

Maurice Jagger (1913–2005)

If you ever shop in the town centre Tesco supermarket, you will be on the same site where various disabled and elderly groups used to get together. Their meeting rooms were upstairs, so one can only imagine the difficulties this presented to those attending. The rooms were in council property, and when the council gave only one month's notice to vacate them, something had to be done to find a new venue. It proved extremely difficult to find somewhere else suitable to meet that would enable elderly and disabled people to gain access easily. There was no money available from the NHS or council, so after consulting with the various organisations involved,

Maurice Jagger Centre.

Maurice launched an appeal to raise the £30,000 needed for a purpose-built property. He found a site opposite the present bus station and the result was the Maurice Jagger Centre, which was built in 1982. It is still used by hundreds of people each week and is the venue for many different groups. Sadly, the only financial help the centre receives comes from what they manage to raise themselves.

Born in Halifax in November 1913, throughout most of his very long life Maurice Jagger devoted his energies to helping others. He always had a deep-seated concern for the welfare of the physically handicapped and was involved with the Halifax Association for the Disabled, as well as many other local and voluntary organisations. He is probably best remembered through the Maurice Jagger Centre mentioned above. He still worked as a volunteer there when he was in his late eighties.

Maurice Jagger was full of energy right from his childhood. He played football for his junior school; he was so good at the sport that he was playing for Halifax Town FC by the time he was eighteen. His first job was in his uncle's firm as an apprentice slater and plasterer. His ambition led him to then join a larger company so that he could benefit from the more comprehensive experience it would offer him. At twenty-five he could have become a professional footballer, such was his skill in the game. Instead he decided to set up his own construction company. Twelve years later he was elected to the borough council where he represented his constituents for the next twenty-eight years. In 1972 he became mayor and, with money raised during his term of office, he set up a Mobile Physiotherapy Unit, which enabled patients to be treated at home. He was made a Freeman of Halifax the following year – an honorary, ceremonial award bestowed in recognition of exceptional service. In view of all the work he had done over the years for so many of the town's residents and charities, it was well deserved.

It was during his term of office as mayor that the foundations were laid for Halifax and Aachen to become twin towns. It began with a letter from the German city's council officials asking if some of them could pay a visit to see how local government was organised in our country. The connection was probably made because of Maurice's earlier visits to Aachen. He had taken apprentices to the town on a number of occasions in the 1950s to help rebuild the city. Bearing in mind that this was not all that long after the Second World War had finished, many parts of the German city were pretty well ruined. No doubt he had got to know like-minded people during that time, which explains why he was approached for that initial visit. And that link with the German city was strengthened with the later foundation of the Halifax Aachen Society.

He married Mary Crapper in 1937 and they had two daughters; Mary died in 2003.

I'd love to have been able to start this piece by saying that Joseph Jagger, the man who broke the bank at Monte Carlo, was from the same family as the much loved and respected philanthropist who gave so much help to the people of Halifax in various ways. But I am informed by his daughter that there is no connection to the Bradford textile engineer who actually did break Monte Carlo's casino bank.

Minster

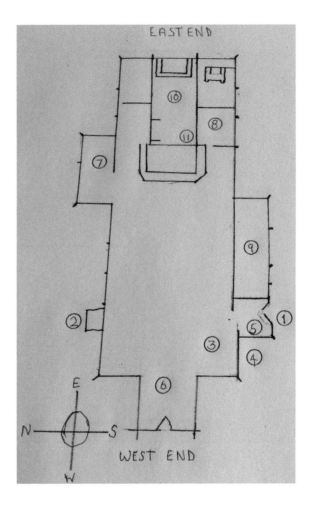

Halifax Minster plan. (Bob Wood)

Numbers in brackets in the text = numbers on the diagram of the church.

In 2009 Halifax Parish Church was designated a minster by the Bishop of Wakefield. The term 'minster' has been around since the seventh century and originally referred to monasteries, and indeed Halifax Parish Church has an early association with Cluniac monks who had probably built a church here by the early twelfth century. As time went on, the term 'minster' gradually came to refer to very long-established churches whose parishes were significantly larger than those around it. Established over 900 years ago, this certainly applies to Halifax Minster, whose parish stretched for over 124 square miles in the Middle Ages.

Its full title is the Minster Church of St John the Baptist, Halifax. People who knew the church in the Middle Ages were of the firm belief that the saint's head, or at least his face, was buried beneath the building. Hence the name.

The minster is well worth a visit as there is plenty to hold your interest, even if you don't have religious beliefs. The entrance used these days used to be reserved solely for use by the gentry (1). Those lower down the social scale had to enter the church through a door on the north side (2). In the late seventeenth century special permission was given to Old Tristram, a licensed beggar, to linger in the church grounds near the south entrance. The hope was that some of the rich upper classes of the town would take pity on him and be generous. There is a life-sized wooden statue of him just inside the church, in front of the first column you come to (3). It was carved in around 1701 by John Aked and is holding the apt message 'Pray remember the poor'.

Before you actually enter the church, take a look at the gravestones just to the left of the entrance, right beside the wall. One of them belongs to John Logan who died on 29 December 1830 (4). There is quite a long inscription from which we learn that he was married twice. His first wife bore him eight children – not unusual in those days. But his poor second wife had twenty-four children by him. You have to wonder how on earth he managed to feed and clothe his thirty-two offspring, and how many of them survived into adulthood.

Next, step in the porch. Just beyond the glass doors there is a twelfth-century grave cover (5), which has a pair of cropper's shears carved into it. Given how old the grave cover is, it indicates just how long the textile industry has been going on in the area.

Suspended above the font at the west end of the church is a beautifully carved, fifteenth-century font cover (6). Font covers of one kind or another were compulsory from

Minster south entrance. (Tom Threlfall)

1236 and actually did sit on top of fonts in order to prevent people pinching the holy water it held. There would always be some contained in the font, since at that time the water was only changed once a year on Easter Sunday. The cover you see in the minster now wasn't always plain; it was originally brightly painted, as many of them were back then. During the time of the Civil War it was hidden away to prevent the puritanical Roundheads destroying it when they took over control of the town in 1644. The information leaflet available in the church states that the font cover was hidden in a house owned by a member of the church while the Roundheads remained in Halifax. However, I was told by one of the volunteers on duty during my visit that it was hidden in the cellar of the Ring O' Bells pub opposite the minster. Either way, by the time it was reinstalled in the church the paint had all worn off – hence the plain unpainted font cover we see today.

There are three chapels inside the church. Going clockwise and starting on the north wall is the Rokeby Chapel (7), which was built in 1533. This is dedicated to William Rokeby, vicar of Halifax from 1502 to 1521. Following his death his heart and bowels were encased in a lead casket and buried beneath the chancel (which is at the east end of the church, where the choir stalls are). When the chantry chapel was built in his memory, his remains were transferred there. It is interesting to note that he officiated at the baptism of Mary Tudor (Bloody Mary) on 20 February 1516 when she was just two days old. It was customary at that time to christen babies very quickly after they were born due to the high mortality rate of infants.

Cross to the opposite side of the church and you come to the Wellington Chapel (8). This was originally the Chapel of the Resurrection, but was adopted by the Duke of Wellington's Regiment, rededicated in 1951 and became their regimental chapel. Be sure to look closely at the chairs in the chapel and see how many mice you can spot carved into the legs. These chairs are by Robert Thompson's Craftsmen Ltd, whose founder was the world-renowned 'Mouseman', a mouse carved on his pieces being his trademark, a tradition that continues today.

The next and last chapel is the Holdsworth Chapel (9), dedicated to the memory of his father by Robert Holdsworth, the church's vicar from 1525 to 1556, who, although he was from a wealthy family, is described as a pluralist. In other words, despite his wealth and the privilege it brought him, he nonetheless believed in tolerance towards everyone – highborn or lowborn.

His family home was what is now an independent hotel and restaurant – Holdsworth House. Sadly, he was murdered on 8 May 1556 when thieves broke into his vicarage late at night during the latest of many break-ins to the vicarage during his time there.

And don't forget to look up. Above the chancel there are a number of beautiful painted ceiling panels (10). Remember John Aked who carved the statue of Old Tristram, whom I mentioned earlier? Well he and James Hoyle painted them, and the panels have been there since around 1695–1703. They were repainted in the 1820s and were cleaned after the Second World War.

When you have finished looking up, look down for a bit while you are still standing in the chancel. Against the rood screen, which separates the nave from the chancel, there are six fifteenth-century misericords (11). Below each seat are various carvings, including a 'green man'.

There is so much to see in our minster that I could go on for much longer, but I can thoroughly recommend a visit – just make sure you give yourself plenty of time to look round.

Mulcture Hall

Next time you are in Bankfield Museum and find yourself in the Duke of Wellington's Regiment museum area, take a minute to look at the ceiling. It is a fine seventeenth-century plaster ceiling and it wasn't always there. At one time it lived in the Mulcture Hall built by John Smithson, a building with walls that were 3 feet (91.5 cm) thick. At that time the hall was the place where the money was collected, which people had to pay to have their corn ground for them.

A report about Halifax had been prepared in 1851 by a visiting civil engineer and sanitary inspector called William Ranger, following the introduction of the Public Health Act in 1848. He had been invited to come by the town's General Board of Health to advise what steps needed to be taken to comply with the Act.

Formerly in Mulcture Hall.

He focussed on the area from around Dean Clough down to and including Winding Road, just behind where the bus station is now. He also looked at Northowram, Southowram and parts of Haley Hill. He was shocked by what he found; for example, there was an instance where 120 people shared one toilet!

He submitted a report to the General Board of Health, strongly encouraging them to take urgent steps to comply with the Public Health Act as soon as possible. This resulted in a flurry of reservoirs being built so that a decent water supply could be provided, particularly to the working-class areas of the town. Ranger himself planned drainage and sewer networks in 1853, all of which emptied into the Hebble Brook below Water Lane Bridge. It was to be another fifty years before a proper sewage treatment works was opened in Salterhebble.

As a direct result of Ranger's report, parts of Mulcture Hall were converted for use as a lodging house by John Crossley, the carpet manufacturer and philanthropist. It included a kitchen, dormitories, a wash house, a reading room and provided shelter for fifty men at a cost of 3*d* per night (less than £3 in today's money).

Mulcture Hall probably stood on Mulcture Hall Lane (behind Sainsbury's). Sadly, it fell into disrepair and was demolished in 1937.

Mulcture Hall Road now.

Nature Reserves

There are over 1,400 Local Nature Reserves (LNRs) in England. These are areas designated under Section 21 of the National Parks and Access to the Countryside Act 1949 by local authorities such as Calderdale, but parish and town councils can also declare LNRs provided they have been given the necessary power by their local authority. In and around Halifax we have six LNRs.

One of them is Ogden Water, which was designated as an LNR in 2003. It is well known to many of the town's residents as somewhere to go for a nice walk or a picnic.

Ogden Water has supplied the area with water for well over a century.

But more than that, the moors above it form part of a Special Protection Area, which is of international importance for breeding birds.

Although it has been used by local people for the past 100 years or more (folk strolled across the dam wall at one time, and still do), the whole area was only officially opened to the public in 1987 by Yorkshire Water. If you manage to get up through the woods to the higher ground, on a clear day you will be able to see as far as the Peak District in Derbyshire and Selby in North Yorkshire.

A clue as to what the area looked like some centuries ago comes from its name. 'Ogden' is derived from the Old English word *okendene*, meaning 'oak valley'. The wooded area was originally smaller than it is today, but was gradually extended over the course of the nineteenth and twentieth centuries, and the type of trees within it have also changed. Now you will see a mixture of conifers and broadleafed woodland.

The reservoir itself is fed by streams running through Ogden Clough and Skirden Clough, both watercourses originating on Ogden Moor. The water then makes its way down, eventually joining the Hebble Brook.

For some time it was thought that part of the Roman road from Manchester to Ilkley passed across the north end of the reservoir. But recent archaeological excavations

Dam wall – the only place where people could walk originally.

have led to the conclusion that it might not have been Roman at all but medieval, due to its construction and lack of ditches. On the other hand, some of the road was destroyed when the reservoir was made. So the jury is still out at the time of writing.

Construction of the reservoir started in 1854 and was finished in 1858, but it was not without its problems. These were caused originally way back in the Ice Age due to action on the landscape by glaciers. The end result affecting nineteenth-century construction of the reservoir was that any water being held in it would leak out through the very fractured rock forming the area meant to contain it. So the engineer, J. F. Bateman, got round the problem by lining the entire bottom of the dam with a blanket of clay, thus making it watertight. This solution is unique among large reservoirs worldwide.

There are over 130 different species of birds to be seen here. Down on the reservoir you can always see the ubiquitous mallards, as well as dippers, herons and great crested grebes – and keep your eyes open for kingfishers along the streams. During the summer months the swallows, house martins and swifts skim across the water searching for insect snacks. Winter visitors include goldeneyes, goosanders and Canada geese.

Ogden Water from the western side.

Keep your eyes open for wildlife in the woods around Ogden Water. (Diane Holloway)

Beyond the reservoir and into the woodland you could well spot robins, chaffinches, great tits, goldfinches, gold crests, both green and great spotted woodpeckers, jays and bullfinches, depending on the time of year. Where woodland and moorland are next to each other you may well see crossbills in autumn, while winter brings thrushes, redwings and fieldfares to the nearby fields. The moors support curlew and red grouse and if you are lucky you might even see twites, wheatears and merlins, plus long- and short-eared owls. If you are really fortunate you might also see some roe deer and foxes, but grey squirrels and rabbits are common and easy to spot. If you are still in the park on a summer evening you will be able to see bats hunting the many insects that also populate the area.

Watch where you walk though or you might easily trample flowers such as pink purslane, common spotted orchid and wood sorrel among many other flora to be seen.

Other nature reserves around Halifax include Cromwell Bottom, Norland Moor, Long Wood and Scar Wood.

Oliver Smithies

A Nobel Prize winner attended Copley Primary School on the outskirts of Halifax. Oliver Smithies won this prestigious award in 2007 for his work in genetics, which he was awarded jointly with two other scientists. The Nobel Prize was for 'Physiology or Medicine' and the citation states it was 'for their discoveries of principles for introducing specific gene modifications in mice by the use of embryonic stem cells'.

Born and raised in Halifax, while at Copley Primary School he had a bout of rheumatic fever when he was seven years old. This precluded him from joining in

Above left: Oliver Smithies. (Courtesy of Mapos under Creative Commons 2.0)

Above right: Oliver Smithies, with the American Institute of Chemists Gold Medal. (Douglas A. Lockard, Science History Institute)

sports activities, so he turned to books instead. He went on to Heath Grammar School (now Crossley Heath School) from 1936 to 1943 and from there to Balliol College, Oxford, where he initially read medicine. He graduated with a first-class BA in animal physiology, including biochemistry. He went on to take a post-graduate degree in biochemistry, receiving his DPhil in 1951. He believed that his love of science came from an early fascination with radios and telescopes.

On the advice of his tutor at Oxford, he reluctantly applied for a visiting fellowship at the University of Wisconsin–Madison in the USA after receiving his DPhil. However, he had a problem with acquiring a US visa, despite being awarded a Commonwealth Fund fellowship to take up the post when it was offered to him. He therefore spent seven years in Canada, working at the Connaught Medical Research Laboratory at the University of Toronto. While there he found twenty-five proteins in the blood, whereas prior to his research it was believed there were only five.

He was finally able to go to the University of Wisconsin–Madison in 1960, where he became Professor of Genetics and Medical Genetics. Here he pursued his interest in finding a way to replace the gene responsible for sickle-cell disease with a normal gene. His work in this area paved the way for other research scientists to do further work in the field of gene therapy.

By the 1990s he had become a naturalised US citizen and had moved to North Carolina where he held the post of Excellence Professor of Pathology and Laboratory Medicine at the University of North Carolina. He worked daily in his laboratory there until he was in his eighties. He did return to Halifax for a brief visit in 2010, when he unveiled a commemorative plaque at his old primary school in Copley. A true inspiration for the children there.

He died on 10 January 2017 at the age of ninety-one, having won many awards over the course of his life, as well as being elected to the United States National Academy of Sciences, among other prestigious institutions and receiving honorary degrees from three universities.

Pestilence

Although the most recent suspected, but unconfirmed, case of the Black Death (plague) in the UK was in 2014/15, this deadly disease first reached Yorkshire in 1349. By December of the same year it had already wiped out around a third of the population of Britain, and a second vicar of Halifax had been claimed by the disease some weeks earlier. Following further epidemics in 1369 and 1375, it is thought that there were only around 220 people left in Halifax. It didn't help that Yorkshire as a whole had been affected earlier by famine between 1315 and 1322, due to very poor weather affecting the harvests. So people would have already been in a weakened state and therefore more susceptible to catching any disease going.

Sadly, plague returned to Halifax several times over the next few centuries, claiming over 500 lives in 1645. Things got so bad that year, that £66 13s 4d (over £39,000 in today's money) was allotted to the town to help alleviate the situation for its poverty-stricken survivors.

Quality Street

J. M. Barrie is best known for writing *Peter Pan*, but before that was published one of his lesser-known plays had its premier on 11 November 1901. It was called *Quality Street* and became the inspiration for the name of a tin of chocolates that was launched in 1936 and was to achieve worldwide fame, and huge sales for its manufacturers.

A few days after John and Violet Mackintosh were married in 1890, they bought a shop in King Cross Lane. It wasn't long before John realised that by far their busiest day was Saturday, so he gave some thought as to how he could capitalise on that. At the time, 'toffee' referred mainly to brittle, sugary boiled sweets, but John wanted a different kind of confectionary from that presently available. So Violet developed

Quality Street poster on the factory where they are made. (Tom Threlfall)

a new recipe. She blended traditional butterscotch with soft American caramel, thus creating a substance that was neither too hard nor too soft; the initial batch weighed 4.5 kg. At the time it was popular to include all sorts of flavourings in sweets and toffee, but it was decided to leave the taste of Violet's invention as natural as possible and not add anything to it. 'Mackintosh's Celebrated Toffee' was born, and so was the beginning of the Mackintosh's Toffee empire.

John Mackintosh was an astute entrepreneur and his business grew rapidly. By 1903 his toffee products were being exported to Italy, Spain and China and the following year a factory was opened in the USA. In 1908 his son Harold joined the company, taking over completely after his father's death in 1920. Then came the product that was revolutionary at the time – Quality Street.

Chocolate was a very expensive luxury in the 1930s and the ordinary person could not afford it. But they could afford toffee. Mackintosh's came up with the innovation of covering their toffee with a thin layer of chocolate, thus putting this previously luxury commodity within the financial reach of working-class families. Not only that, but in order to make their product even more attractive to its prospective customers it was decided to wrap each toffee in brightly coloured paper and put them all in a

Major Quality and Miss Sweetly. (Bob Wood)

tin box, rather than cardboard. This was a marketing ploy, rather than for reasons of economy. A tin box would retain the confectionary's aroma much better, so that the wonderful smell of its contents would waft out whenever the tin was opened, rather than gradually seeping out through cardboard.

These days the tins are decorated to highlight the many different types of sweets they contain, but originally they showed two characters – Major Quality and Miss Sweetly. Their poses changed frequently, and the portraits were designed to suit the country and market the tins were destined for. An exhibition of the various tin designs across the decades reflecting the many different countries the product was sold in was held at the Bankfield Museum in 2018. The number of different tins and poses of the two characters on them was quite astonishing.

Quality Street is still produced in Halifax, even though the business is now owned by Nestlé.

On display at Bankfield Museum. (Bob Wood)

Railways

These days Halifax railway station has two platforms, a ticket hall, a small shop and a waiting room. But at one time it was such a busy station it needed six platforms. There were also ladies' and gentlemens' waiting rooms for first-class passengers, as well as a stationmaster's office, a busy parcels office, a telegraph office, refreshment rooms (note the plural) and a staff canteen. In addition to all these passenger facilities, according to *Railway Memories: No. 11 Halifax & the Calder Valley* there were 'three sizeable goods yards, coal and wagonload sidings, a cattle dock and the coal drops down to road level', plus various cranes and a large warehouse. As well as the

Platform at modern Halifax railway station. (Tom Threlfall)

obvious need to transport the confectionery and woollen goods manufactured in the town, freight traffic also consisted of coal and container goods.

It took a while for Halifax town centre to get a railway at all because it was 200 feet higher than the valley below. And when the railway finally did arrive, it was sited on the 'wrong' side of town from a business viewpoint. Most trade was done with Manchester, but the most convenient site, as far as the train companies were concerned, was on the eastern side. This was due to the gradient the engines had to climb in order to get into the town in the first place.

The first station was at Shaw Syke (a temporary wooden station), around 220 yards west of the present station. It opened on 1 July 1844, later becoming the goods yard mentioned earlier. Six years later a new station was opened, which was designed by Manchester architect Thomas Butterworth. But in 1885 it, and indeed the station building itself, was altered by William Hunt, the Lancashire and Yorkshire Railway's regional architect. That later building is now Grade II listed and is the one you can see when you look down towards Eureka from the road leading to the modern station.

As you travel from Halifax station heading towards Bradford, you enter a tunnel almost immediately and travel through it for 1,105 yards. This is Beacon Hill Tunnel, which was built between 1846 and 1849 and actually opened in 1852. In the same year the next tunnel you pass through was also opened; Wyke Tunnel is even longer at 1,365 yards.

On a lighter note, in the early days of the railway, excursion trains were often run. This resulted in some men dressing up as women to try to take advantage of the cheaper fares the fairer sex had available to them on these trips.

Old railway station building. (Tom Threlfall)

S

Sithee at the Waggoners – Chartism in Halifax

The Waggoners pub in Skircoat Green is now better known as the Standard of Freedom. The area was a magnet for people with radical thoughts – a stalwart of the suffragette movement lived not too far from the pub much later on. But at the time of the name change, the pub was a popular meeting place for Chartists. The landlord was

Formerly called The Waggoners.

Not just dog walkers, cyclists and ramblers, but Chartists too.

sympathetic to the movement and is said to have announced, 'The people of Skircoat Green shall join in that march of freedom. I will raise the standard of freedom at this inn.' Hence the new name.

Chartism had its beginnings in 1836, but was at its height between 1838 and 1848. It was grounded in the working class, whose aim was to achieve for themselves more political rights and influence than they currently had. To this end they devised a People's Charter and their popular name of Chartists was derived from this. Five of their six aims have now been achieved, but originally they were seen as ludicrous demands and strongly resisted by those in power. What they wanted was: (1) A vote for every man aged twenty-one years and over, of sound mind, and not undergoing punishment for a crime; (2) A secret ballot to protect the voter when exercising his vote; (3) No property qualification for Members of Parliament so that constituencies could actually return the man of their choice (see comment below); (4) Payment of Members, enabling anyone, rich or poor, to become an MP and not have to worry about lack of income; (5) Equal constituencies, securing the same amount of representation for the same number of electors, instead of allowing less populous constituencies to have as much or more weight than larger ones; (6) Annual Parliamentary elections, the intention being to make bribery and intimidation very much more difficult and costly.

Point 3 affected the vote for Ernest Jones when he stood as a Radical candidate at Halifax in the 1848 election. Not many of his supporters could comply with the need to own property, so not enough of them could vote and he was not elected.

A petition signed by 1.3 million working people was presented to the House of Commons in 1839, but MPs refused to hear the petitioners. This caused so much anger that in some places, including the West Riding of Yorkshire, a general strike was seriously considered.

Three years later a second petition with over 3 million signatures was presented to Parliament, which was again rejected. This caused such fury among Chartist supporters that a wave of strikes and riots ensued, including what are known as the Plug Riots in Halifax. People from surrounding areas joined with those in Halifax,

Plug rioters threatened the mills. (Tom Threlfall)

all of them intent on stopping production in as many mills as they could. The plan was to remove the plugs from the steam boilers, making them very dangerous to use. These plugs were not at all similar to the plug in your bath; effectively they were the last line of defence in controlling the build-up of steam, and if removed the result could be an explosion of enough force to wreck the factory.

It was estimated by the local newspaper of the time that something like 25,000 people thronged the town's streets at one point. They certainly achieved their objective, since those mills that did not have plugs removed from their boilers by the rioters were so worried about possible violence that they closed up anyway.

The following day brought disaster when an intimidating crowd gathered outside Ackroyd mills at Haley Hill. The cavalry were called in and they charged and fired shots into the crowd, wounding three men in the process. They also took over thirty prisoners.

The final petition to Parliament had 6 million signatures (although many were found to be fake – the real number being around 2 million) and was presented in 1848. As the French king had been deposed earlier in the year, and revolutions were

Chartists dispersed by gunfire and a sabre charge near North Bridge. (Tom Threlfall)

beginning to break out elsewhere in Europe, British authorities were more than a bit concerned. A planned peaceful procession to the House of Commons from a Chartist meeting in London to deliver the petition was therefore banned. So it was delivered to its destination in three horse-drawn cabs.

It is worth mentioning that the Chartist movement was very well supported by women, despite it often being portrayed as mainly for men. This is probably because the charter called for universal suffrage for men only. Getting universal suffrage for women was left to the suffragists and, later on, the more militant and better known suffragettes.

In some respects it could be said that the Chartists failed to achieve their objective, since none of their petitions were accepted by Parliament. However, today the only point that hasn't passed into law is the request to have elections held annually.

T

'The Dukes' – The Duke of Wellington's Regiment (West Riding)

The regiment is held in such high regard by the people of Halifax these days that it's hard to realise we once didn't want anything at all to do with them.

Back in 1873, a petition objecting to their depot being moved to the town was very strongly supported. It was signed by around a quarter of the population and presented to the Secretary of State for War. It seems that Halifax folk were worried about the effect of soldiers in the town and that it would lead, among other things, to 'demoralisation and immorality'. Not everyone agreed with this, especially Edward Ackroyd (local mill owner and philanthropist who lived at Bankfield House) who led

A remarkable tribute to The Dukes.

At the top of The Woolshops.

the support for welcoming the regiment to Halifax; they also handed a petition to the Secretary of State for War, but two days earlier than the one against the depot.

Another eminent supporter was the vicar of Halifax parish church, Revd Charles Musgrave. Such was his enthusiasm, he donated the land on which they then built their Wellesley Barracks. Construction started in early 1875 and all was ready for the army to move in by August 1877. It was to be eighty-two years before they moved out again in 1959. Although they arrived as three different units, they were amalgamated in 1881 and the Duke of Wellington's (West Riding) Regiment was born, after a brief spell as the Halifax Regiment. Rebuilding and modernisation took place fifty-five years later following a fire in the officers' mess. This brought with it the installation of electricity and showers.

The Dukes were given the Freedom of Halifax on 18 June 1945 – 130 years to the day after the Battle of Waterloo, the Duke of Wellington's most famous victory. He commanded the Allied forces in Belgium at that time, which included the 33rd Regiment of Foot, whom Wellington had commanded in 1793. Following various amalgamations, they eventually became the Duke of Wellington's Regiment (West Riding). They were held in high esteem even before the Battle of Waterloo. Earlier in that year Sir Henry Clinton, inspector general of infantry of Wellington's army in Flanders had said of the 33rd: 'Upon the whole I consider this regiment to be in the most advanced state of any in the army.' High praise indeed. When the British squares held firm against attack after attack by his cavalry, Napoleon is supposed to have commented, 'These dogs of English never know when they are beaten.' I suppose that's why we won and he didn't!

The Dukes have had a number of nicknames, one of which appears on the statue erected at the Market Street end of The Woolshops in May 2019. That name is 'The Havercake Lads', which came into use around the time of the American War of Independence (1775–83). A havercake was a sort of flatbread and was traditionally cooked in some parts of the Yorkshire and Pennine area (and still is occasionally). It is made from oatmeal, flour, milk and water that is left overnight and cooked next day. These breads would sometimes be folded and carried in bags to be eaten later, and the bags gave rise to the word haversack. Presumably, the soldiers of the 33rd Regiment continued to make their havercakes when they were deployed to America to fight the rebels there.

The name 'havercake' has its roots in the Norse language. Some centuries later Timothy Taylor's Brewery produced Havercake Ale, which they brewed in 2002 to mark The Dukes' 300-year anniversary. Incidentally, one of the brewery's employees, Arthur Poulter, was awarded the Victoria Cross in the First World War and is mentioned in the section about VCs elsewhere in this book.

In 2006 the proposed amalgamation of the Duke of Wellington's Regiment with the Green Howards and the Prince of Wales's Own Regiment to form the Yorkshire

Representing service in India and The Dukes' family support.

Detail from the Honorary Queen's
Colour in Bankfield Museum.
(Bob Wood)

Regiment became fact. This gave rise to the idea of a memorial for the regiment and, after some consideration of where it should be sited, it was agreed that the centre of Halifax would be the best place, given our past close links. A list of what the organising committee wanted the memorial to reflect was drawn up and the sculptor Andrew Sinclair was commissioned to do the job. His work has featured in worldwide collections, and he has caught the spirit and history of The Dukes perfectly through his magnificent sculpture. Some aspects of the sculpture may be a little puzzling if you are unfamiliar with the regiment's history, but it is worth noting that soldiers from the eighteenth, nineteenth and twentieth centuries are all represented. The elephant reflects the service of the 76th of Foot (later to become 2nd Battalion the Duke of Wellington's Regiment) during the eighteenth century when India became part of the British Empire. Next to the elephant there's a woman and two young children, who represent the families of soldiers who took part in the Second World War, but also serves to illustrate the support given by army families of all those who served in the regiment and who remained in Yorkshire supporting their loved ones. Another couple of interesting features are that all the soldiers have been given the same nose as the Duke of Wellington; if you look closely you can also see that all the soldiers smoke, even if you have to look hard to see a packet of cigarettes tucked into a pocket, or the outline of a cigarette case (inside a pocket). See if you can spot them.

Town Twinning

The very earliest evidence of town twinning was many centuries ago in AD 836 between Paderborn in Germany and Le Mans in France. Modern town twinning started in the 1920s, with 'sister' relationships beginning even earlier in the twentieth century. After the Second World War, these ideas grew to encourage both cultural and commercial links with other countries. Halifax is twinned with Aachen in Germany.

Aachen is the westernmost city in Germany and is also known as Aix-la-Chapelle to the French and some English people. Ownership of the town bounced back and forward over the last few centuries between France and Germany – hence the two names. It is located near the borders with Belgium and the Netherlands in a former coal-mining area. Like Halifax, manufacturing was once a major industry in Aachen's economy, but today textile production makes up only 10 per cent of total manufacturing jobs in the city.

The first exchange visit between Halifax and Aachen took place in 1949 and exchange visits have taken place each year since then. We have been legally twinned with Aachen since 14 November 1979.

Other town twinning relationships in the Halifax area are: Todmorden is twinned with Bramsche, Germany, and Roncq, France; Brighouse is twinned with Lüdenscheid, Germany; Elland is twinned with Riorges, France; Hebden Bridge is twinned with Warstei, Germany and Saint-Pol-sur-Ternoise, France.

Halifax is proud of its association with Aachen. (Paul Hadfield)

Under a Night Sky – Edward Crossley's Telescopes

The Crossley family is best known for producing carpets at their Dean Clough factory. But Edward Crossley, Joseph Crossley's eldest son and heir, also had a deep interest in astronomy. He was a Fellow of the Royal Astronomical Society from 1867 and his paper 'Observations of Mars during the Opposition of 1900–1901' was published in the society's monthly journal.

Bermerside, now private apartments.

Bermerside, his home in Skircoat Green, is now an apartment block. But originally it was the site for the well-equipped observatory he had constructed in his garden. However, it turned out there was a problem that prevented him being able to look at the stars successfully. It wasn't light pollution, as it would be in Skircoat Green today, it was hazy air pollution from the town's many factories.

One of his telescopes was originally located in another back garden. It came from London and had belonged to Andrew Ainslie Common – another amateur astronomer who was one of the earliest astrophotographers. It was a 36 inch (910 mm) reflecting telescope (a telescope in which a mirror is used to collect and focus light). It seems that the big reflector in Crossley's telescope was a bit ahead of its time and later telescopes with very large reflectors were successfully used in the 1900s.

In the end, Edward Crossley decided to give that telescope to the Lick Observatory in California in 1895, since he wasn't able to use it in Halifax. It was still being used 115 years later when it was involved in the search for extra-solar planets in 2010. But that was its last job, as it had to be taken out of service. This was not due to any part of it being broken, but because of budget cuts.

Another of his telescopes is still being used regularly, even though it is over 150 years old. It is known as the Thomas Cooke telescope, and is a refractor telescope, which means it uses a lens such as you would find in a camera. It was made in 1867 by

Edward Crossley's telescope is now here, in the Lick Observatory. (Courtesy of Michael from San Jose, California, under Creative Commons)

Thomas Cooke & Sons – an instrument-making firm, not the travel agents. It is installed in the Space Place at Carter Observatory, Wellington, New Zealand. This is a public museum and planetarium with a focus on space and New Zealand astronomy. Visitors can use Crossley's telescope in the evenings to gaze into deep space. It got there after Edward Crossley's death, when it was bought by Revd Dr David Kennedy, a New Zealand vicar with a keen interest in astronomy. He built an observatory at Meeanee, near Napier on New Zealand's North Island, and used Edward Crossley's telescope to take photographs of Halley's Comet in 1910. It was then purchased by Wellington City Council in 1923 and taken to Wellington before being transferred to the Carter Observatory, where it has been put to very good use ever since.

V

Vagabonds, Beggars and the Like

Mention that you come from Halifax and people who are not from here often misquote part of a poem called 'Beggars Litany', written in the early seventeenth century by John Taylor. 'From Hull, Hell and Halifax, good Lord deliver us' they say. The poem in full is as follows:

> There is a proverb and a prayer withall,
> That we may not to three strange places fall;
> From Hull, from Hell, from Halifax, 'tis this,
> From all these three, Good Lord, deliver us.
> This praying proverb's meaning to set down,
> Men do not wish deliverance from the town;
> The town's named Kingston, Hull's the furious river;
> And from Halifax's dangers, I say, Lord, deliver.
> At Halifax, the law so sharp doth deal,
> That whoso more than 13 pence doth steal;
> They have a gyn that wondrous, quick and well,
> Sends thieves all headless unto Heaven or Hell.
> From Hell each man says Lord, deliver me.
> Because from Hell can no redemption be.
> Men may escape from Hull and Halifax,
> But sure in Hell, there is not heavier tax.
> Let each one for themselves in this agree,
> And pray – from Hell, Good Lord, deliver me.

Reading the complete poem puts a rather different complexion on the familiar saying. It is the River Hull that should give cause for concern, not the town of Kingston-upon-Hull. There's also a theory that in this case 'Hell' is a corruption of Hallam, and not the opposite of Heaven, as Sheffield had a gibbet and at the time this poem was written Sheffield was in the county of Hallamshire. However, their gibbet did not have a blade, but was a gallows-like structure used to hang the dead or

Spare some change?

dying bodies of criminals. They were hung there as warning to others who might be considering taking up a life of crime.

A well-known beggar in eighteenth-century Halifax was Old Tristram, whose statue in the minster is mentioned elsewhere in this book. Local historian David Glover's research on Old Tristram concluded that he was not a local man originally, but that he settled in Elland in the late 1640s and may have gone there after possibly serving as a soldier in the Civil War. I can't help wondering if he was, perhaps, one of the soldiers who was stationed in the town at some point, since both Royalists and Puritans spent time here and he could have fought with either army. Maybe he liked what he saw, moved his family to the area after the war and then added two more children to those he already had when he got here. The research done by David Glover concludes that 'Old Tristram was the John Trustram ... buried at Halifax on 11 February 1711'. Tristram was not a Christian name in this instance, but a surname that was a corruption of Trusteram.

Throughout our history, vagrants and beggars have not been well tolerated anywhere on the whole, including Halifax, and would have had a hard time of it under various laws going back centuries. For example, towards the end of the reign of Elizabeth I various Acts were passed that meant beggars could be whipped. In 1597, due to a scarcity of corn and the resulting high prices for bread and food generally, plus a high rate of homelessness, it was estimated that there were some 10,000 vagabonds in London and 2,000 in Norwich. And this was even though there had also been a series of Acts passed in the same period that decreed the care of the poor was the community's responsibility. Halifax experienced the same problems and the town probably had its share of beggars and vagabonds too.

Vagabonds were commonly perceived in the past as being gangs of unruly young men who roamed around committing acts of violence and were to be feared. In reality they were usually just one, sometimes two, men, who were often unemployed and were seeking work, or on a trip to visit family members. But they could still find themselves put in the stocks for three days and three nights and only fed bread and water, thanks to the Vagabonds and Beggars Act of 1494. That same Act also stated that beggars should be returned to their home area and be made to stay there. So Old Tristram was fortunate to have been allowed to beg in the precincts of Halifax Parish Church, as the minster was then.

These days begging is still an offence and those who sleep rough or beg in a public place can be arrested under the Vagrancy Act of 1824 even now, but rarely are unless they are drunk or abusive.

Worldwide Halifax

It's not only West Yorkshire that has somewhere called Halifax within its borders. The town's name is to be found in many other parts of the world too – some inhabited, others not.

Lunar Reconnaissance Orbiter captured this image of Earth. (Courtesy of NSSDCA Photo Gallery, NASA Photo ID: AS17-148-22727, under Creative Commons)

Halifax Bay, Queensland, Australia. (Courtesy of Robert Linsdell under Creative Commons)

Australia

There are two places called Halifax in Queensland, Australia. One is a small town of fewer than 500 people and is located on the Herbert River. Like many parts of our town, on occasion it has suffered flooding. In the case of the Australian town, it was in March 2018 following particularly heavy rainfall that caused the Herbert River to overflow and flood many of the town's houses.

Like Halifax, it has a town hall and regular community markets. The land the town stands on was purchased in 1880 by a blacksmith called August Anderssen and then became a sugar plantation, the area being ideally suited to growing that crop.

Just 32 miles away there is also Halifax Bay. It was named by Captain Cook between 6 and 8 June 1770, and the area was originally inhabited by the Warakami and the Wulgurkaba aboriginal tribes. The bay is an important Australian ecological area and is part of the Great Barrier Reef, a World Heritage Area.

Canada

There's a small mountain range with an area of 51 km² on Vancouver Island, which is known as the Halifax Range. There is also a municipality in the province of

Above: Belgian relief ship involved in collision. (Courtesy of David Pattison. This photo is from a booklet published in 1917 and republished in 1918 called *Devastated Halifax* by Gerald E. Wier)

Below: Modern Halifax, Nova Scotia, Canada. (Alexk001 under Creative Commons)

Harbour Nova Scotia around 1960. (Ralph Pattison with permission from his son, David Pattison)

Nova Scotia known as Halifax. Rather like the amalgamation of several towns in the Calderdale Valley that then fell under the jurisdiction of Calderdale Council, Canada's Halifax Regional Municipality was formed by an amalgamation of the former City of Halifax, the City of Dartmouth, the Town of Bedford, and the separate Halifax County Municipality in 1996. Halifax City itself was founded 247 years earlier in 1749 by Colonel Edward Cornwallis.

Disaster struck the town in 1917 when a Belgian relief ship collided with a French munitions ship and 1,800 people were killed in the resultant explosion. Its harbour has several small islands within it, and a small peninsula known as Deadman's Island. It was called that because it is the burial location of some prisoners of war from 1812.

Before we leave Canada, there is one more Halifax to mention: Halifax Parish on Prince Edward Island, which has existed as a civil parish since sometime between 1764 and 1766.

United States

As well as a coastal area and river named Halifax, there are also seven other places in the USA known as Halifax. The river is within the Daytona region of Florida, as is the coastal area of the same name, with some fabulous beaches.

Halifax is an unincorporated community in Allen County, Kentucky ('unincorporated' simply means it is a settlement that is governed as part of a larger administrative division, it does not govern itself).

Halifax, Massachusetts, has a population of approximately 7,700 people and was founded in 1734. It has a mix of rural, agricultural (including cranberry bogs) and residential development.

Halifax, Missouri, is another unincorporated community. It was certainly established by 1888, as that's when it got its own post office, but that was closed again in 1925. It was named after Halifax, Nova Scotia.

Halifax is a town and county located in North Carolina with a total population of over 54,000. Founded in 1757, it was named after the 2nd Earl of Halifax, who became known as 'Father of the Colonies' due to his success in extending American commerce. It is also known as 'the Birthplace of Freedom', being the location for the adoption of the Halifax Resolves, which was the first official action by a colony calling for independence, resulting in a strong movement in the colonies advocating separation from Britain. In a way you can see a link between this American town and our own insofar as independent thought is concerned, with Chartism in the following century in England. It was very strong in our town, although that movement was intended to put pressure on politicians to concede manhood suffrage. It too would give independence to some of its population.

Halifax Township in Pennsylvania had a population of 3,483 according to the 2010 census. Its name comes from Fort Halifax, which was nearby and was a temporary eighteenth-century stronghold during the French and Indian War.

Halifax in Vermont, a small town of around 800 people, is the second oldest town in the state and it too was named in honour of the 2nd Earl of Halifax. It was founded on 11 May 1750.

Halifax in Halifax County, Virginia, is slightly larger than its Vermont counterpart, having a population of just over 1,000. It is on the USA's National Register of Historic Places, which is a 'list of districts, sites, buildings, structures, and objects deemed worthy of preservation for their historical significance'.

Downtown Halifax, North Carolina, USA. (Courtesy of Indy beetle under Creative Commons)

X-rays – Hospital History in Halifax

In 1841 a new workhouse was built in Gibbet Street, which was the forerunner of the local hospital of St John's. It turned out not to be a terribly popular hospital to be treated for your illness, simply because of its former workhouse connection. It was to be 1972 before it was finally demolished.

If you were poor and couldn't afford medical treatment, you could go to Halifax General Dispensary. This was established in Hatters Close in February 1808, with a

Royal Halifax Infirmary, now private apartments.

surgical ward being opened in a cottage nearby in 1825. The idea for supplying free medical help and advice for the poor of the town came from Revd Dr H. W. Coulthurst who was the vicar of Halifax at the time. Health facilities for the poor were desperately needed, but were unaffordable for them otherwise.

A lot of the health problems in the mid-1800s, coupled with high death rates among both infants and adults, were identified by the Health of Towns Commission (concerned with public health in the United Kingdom) as being caused by the lack of a proper sewerage system, together with pollution of the Hebble Brook by the factories sited along it. Terrible housing conditions in the east of the town made matters worse.

The Halifax Infirmary on Free School Lane replaced the Dispensary in 1896; it was formally opened by the Duke and Duchess of York, who would later become King George V and Queen Mary. On the whole, it was financed by public subscriptions. The new hospital was supposed to be called Halifax Royal Infirmary, Queen Victoria having given her permission for 'Royal' to be included. However, the Duke of York got mixed up and opened it as the Royal Halifax Infirmary. In the 1920s some new wards were opened, including one for X-ray. This diagnostic advancement was discovered by a German mechanical engineer and physicist called Wilhelm Conrad Röntgen in 1895. Within less than a year a radiology department was opened in a Glasgow hospital and hospitals around the world were using the technology routinely by the early 1900s. Röntgen became the first person to win the Nobel Prize in physics in 1901.

The new Calderdale Royal Hospital at Salterhebble replaced St Luke's Hospital in 2001.

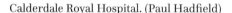

Calderdale Royal Hospital. (Paul Hadfield)

Y

Young Prince John's Halifax Companion

On 12 July 1905 King George V's youngest child was born at Sandringham, Norfolk. Prince John developed epilepsy and at one time it was rumoured that he was kept isolated on the royal estate. But this was far from the truth. It was felt by his family that playmates in his age group would be beneficial for him and one of those found to keep him company was a young Yorkshire lass called Winifred Thomas. Although her name and home county were known about, the connection to Halifax was discovered comparatively recently by local historian, David Glover.

Sandringham, royal residence in Norfolk. (Courtesy of RXUYDC under Creative Commons)

Winifred had been sent to live with her uncle, who worked on the royal estate, when she was around nine or ten to try to improve her health. When it was decided that the young prince would benefit from having a friend of his own age to keep him company, Winifred was suggested as being a suitable companion. She was educated by Prince John's nurse, alongside the young royal.

She stayed at Sandringham until 1918, when she returned to Halifax. Sadly, Prince John died following a massive epileptic fit the following year. Later, Winifred met Leslie Sharpe, whom she married in Calcutta in 1927. She died in 1980 at the age of seventy-five, having returned to England with her husband when he retired in 1959.

Z

Zoo

The first zoo in the world opened in Vienna in 1752; the first in Britain was London Zoo, which opened in April 1828 and was the third in the world to be founded. Halifax had to wait until Whitsuntide 1909 before it too got its own zoo, although a travelling menagerie had visited Halifax in the mid-eighteenth century. The town's Zoological Gardens and Amusement Park was to be found roughly where Chivenedge Crescent and Siddal Rugby Club are now. The park was open from 10 a.m. to 10 p.m. and promised 'a wonderful collection of wild animals and birds, donkey and elephant rides'. As well as the elephant and camel, which had been paraded through Halifax to promote the zoo's opening, the public would be able to see a wide variety of animals including lions, a leopard, bears, zebras, wolves, Arctic foxes, hyenas, monkeys and all sorts of exotic birds, among many other attractions. To make it even more interesting, five wolf cubs had been born the week before the zoo opened, and they were promoted as an added attraction. In September of the same year four polar bears were also born. The zoo was so well publicised that just during the first three days it was open, it had 50,000 visitors who travelled to Halifax from all over Yorkshire. Entry cost 6*d* (over £24 in today's money). However, there were a few problems. When some visitors teased a wild boar, it showed its annoyance by leaping over the 3-foot fence surrounding its enclosure and attacking a nearby woman. Although she hit it with her umbrella, it nonetheless bit her thigh and hands. A plucky young man dragged the animal off and it was finally taken away by zoo staff.

Fortunately, things didn't turn out as badly as they could have done when two bears escaped one Tuesday in June 1913. One was a Russian bear and the other a Canadian grizzly. The Russian bear was captured before it reached the gate however, the grizzly took off down Exley Bank and then turned into Jubilee Road. So instead of Shakespeare's stage direction of 'Exit, pursued by a bear' in *The Winter's Tale*, it was the other way round really. The bear was making the exit pursued by the zoo's head keeper and staff. It sought safety in Elland Wood and managed to avoid the two attempts made to lasso it. After an hour and a half's freedom it decided to make its way down to the canal. Eventually it stepped into a noose that had been laid on the ground. It was then successfully captured and unceremoniously hauled over a wall

A grizzly bear escaped from the zoo. (Bob Wood)

and popped into a waiting van. An elephant also escaped, but decided it wasn't that bothered and fell asleep beneath a tree in the zoo's grounds.

The animals were sold off at the end of the 1916 season, probably to bigger zoos. The First World War would have accounted for a decline in visitors and therefore in income to pay the staff and feed the animals. No doubt, food shortages had an impact and finding enough meat to feed the carnivores or enough silage to feed the ruminants would have been very difficult.

Select Bibliography

Books

Bairstow, Martin, *The Manchester & Leeds Railway: The Calder Valley Line* (Halifax: Martin Bairstow, 1987)

Cossic, Annick and Patrick Galliou (eds), *Spas in Britain and in France in the Eighteenth and Nineteenth Centuries* (Newcastle: Cambridge Scholars Press, 2006)

Hargreaves, John A., *Halifax* (Edinburgh: Edinburgh University Press, 1999)

Hey, David, *The Oxford Companion to Local & Family History* (Oxford: Oxford University Press, 1996)

Hoskins, W. G., *Local History in England* (New York: Longman Inc USA, 1984)

Walker, David E., *Adventure In Diamonds* (London: World Distributors (Manchester) Ltd, 1957)

Whitworth, Alan, *Yorkshire VCs* (Barnsley: Pen & Sword Military, 2012)

Wild, Jack and Stephen Chapman, *Railway Memories: No. 11 Halifax and the Calder Valley* (Todmorden: Bellcode Books, 1998)

Booklets

River Calder Fact File (Environment Agency)

Harkness, Leslie, *How Diamond Polishing Came to Halifax*

Websites

Malcolm Bull's Calderdale Companion, calderdalecompanion.co.uk

Eye on Calderdale, eyeoncalderdale.com/history-of-flooding-in-calderdale

Hebden Bridge Times, hebdenbridgetimes.co.uk/news/when-zoo-animals-roamed-the-streets-1-1807701

The Shopper, halifaxpeople.com/the-opening-of-halifax-zoo.html

National Archives, nationalarchives.gov.uk

The Secret War Report of the OSS by Edward J. Epstein, edwardjayepstein.com/diamond/chap9.htm

Logan Nye, wearethemighty.com/articles/this-top-secret-mission-kept-the-nazis-from-getting-amsterdams-diamonds

Hali-facts Halifax Minster, halifaxminster.org.uk

The Tudor Society, tudorsociety.com/february-1516-birth-christening-mary

Street Angels, halifaxstreetangels.org

Intriguing history, intriguing-history.com/vagabonds-beggars-act

The Conversation, theconversation.com/air-pollution-in-victorian-era-britain-its-effects-on- health-now-revealed-87208

Air Pollution, air-quality.org.uk/02.php

A brief history of Halifax, Nova Scotia, Canada by Tim Lambert, localhistories.org/halifax.html

Encyclopedia of World Biography, encyclopedia.com/people/literature-and-arts/english-literature-1500-1799-biographies/sir-thomas-browne

Museums Sheffield, museums-sheffield.org.uk/blog/2011/10/sheffield's-horrible-history

Halifax Courier, halifaxcourier.co.uk

The Chartist, link.springer.com/chapter/10.1007/978-1-349-16921-4_10 Experience: Studies in Working-Class Radicalism and Culture, 1830–60 pp. 311–344

BBC History, bbc.co.uk

Royal Astronomical Society, academic.oup.com/mnras/article/61/8/561/1246921

Radio Times, radiotimes.com

Biography, biography.com/crime-figure/john-christie